*Published for the Bahá'í World Congress
on the Occasion of the Centenary of the
Ascension of Bahá'u'lláh
and the Inauguration of His Covenant*

---

*Publicado para el Congreso Mundial Bahá'í
en la Ocasión del Centenario de
la Ascensión de Bahá'u'lláh
y de la Inauguración de Su Convenio*

---

*Publiées pour le Congrès mondial Bahá'í à
l'Occasion du Centenaire de
l'Ascension de Bahá'u'lláh
et de l'Inauguration de Son Alliance*

BAHÁ'U'LLÁH

Transform My Spirit
PRAYERS FOR REFLECTION
AND CELEBRATION

Transforma Mi Espíritu
ORACIONES PARA LA REFLEXIÓN
Y LA CELEBRACIÓN

Transforme Mon Âme
PRIÈRES POUR LA RÉFLEXION
ET LA CÉLÉBRATION

CONTENTS

Prayers are reprinted from:

Bahá'í Prayers: A Selection of Prayers Revealed by Bahá'u'lláh, the Báb, and 'Abdu'l-Bahá (Wilmette, Ill.: Bahá'í Publishing Trust, 1991).

Oraciones Bahá'ís: Selección de Oraciones Reveladas por Bahá'u'lláh, el Báb, y 'Abdu'l-Bahá (Argentina: EBILA, 1990).

Prières Bahá'íes: Sélection de prières révélées par le Báb, Bahá'u'lláh, et 'Abdu'l-Bahá (Brussels: Maison d'Éditions Bahá'íes, 1973).

CONTENIDO

TABLE DES MATIÈRES

GENERAL PRAYERS

ORACIONES GENERALES

PRIÈRES GÉNÉRALES

MORNING
AWAKENING TO THE LIGHT OF GOD

MAÑANA
DESPERTÁNDOSE A LA LUZ DE DIOS

MATIN
S'ÉVEILLER À LA LUMIÈRE DE DIEU

I have wakened in Thy shelter, O my God, and it becometh him that seeketh that shelter to abide within the Sanctuary of Thy protection and the Stronghold of Thy defense. Illumine my inner being, O my Lord, with the splendors of the Dayspring of Thy Revelation, even as Thou didst illumine my outer being with the morning light of Thy favor.

—BAHÁ'U'LLÁH

He despertado bajo tu amparo, oh mi Dios, y corresponde a quien busca tal amparo, permanecer dentro del Santuario de tu protección y la Fortaleza de tu defensa. Ilumina mi ser interior, o mi Señor, con los resplandores de la Aurora de tu Revelación, así como iluminaste mi ser exterior con la luz matinal de tu favor.

—BAHÁ'U'LLÁH

Je me suis réveillé dans ton refuge ô mon Dieu, et il convient à celui qui cherche cet abri de demeurer dans le sanctuaire de ta protection et dans la forteresse de ta défense. Illumine mon être intérieur, ô mon Dieu, par la splendeur de l'Aurore de ta révélation, comme tu as illuminé mon être extérieur par la lumière matinale de tes bienfaits.

—BAHÁ'U'LLÁH

QUICKENING THE SPIRITUAL NATURE

REVIVIENDO LA NATURALEZA ESPIRITUAL

RANIMER LA NATURE SPIRITUELLE

My God, my Adored One, my King, my Desire! What tongue can voice my thanks to Thee? I was heedless, Thou didst awaken me. I had turned back from Thee, Thou didst graciously aid me to turn towards Thee. I was as one dead, Thou didst quicken me with the water of life. I was withered, Thou didst revive me with the heavenly stream of Thine utterance which hath flowed forth from the Pen of the All-Merciful.

O Divine Providence! All existence is begotten by Thy bounty; deprive it not of the waters of Thy generosity, neither do Thou withhold it from the ocean of Thy mercy. I beseech Thee to aid and assist me at all times and under all conditions, and seek from the heaven of Thy grace Thine ancient favor. Thou art, in truth, the Lord of bounty, and the Sovereign of the kingdom of eternity.

—BAHÁ'U'LLÁH

¡Mi Dios, mi Adorado, mi Rey, mi Deseo! ¿Qué lengua puede expresar mis gracias a Ti? Yo era negligente, Tú me despertaste. Yo me había alejado de Ti. Tú bondadosamente me ayudaste a volver hacia Ti. Yo era como un muerto, Tú me vivificaste con el agua de vida. Yo estaba marchito, Tú me reanimaste con la corriente celestial de tu palabra que ha fluido de la Pluma del Todo Misericordioso.

¡Oh Divina Providencia! Toda la existencia es engendrada por tu munificencia; no la prives de las aguas de tu generosidad, ni del océano de tu misericordia. Te imploro que me ayudes y me asistas en todo momento y en todas las condiciones, y anhelo tu antiguo favor del cielo de tu gracia. Tú eres, en verdad, el Señor de bondad y el Soberano del reino de la eternidad.

—BAHÁ'U'LLÁH

Mon Dieu, mon adoré, mon roi, mon désir! Quelle langue peut exprimer ma gratitude à ton égard? J'étais insouciant, Tu m'as éveillé. Je m'étais détourné de Toi, Tu m'as aidé par ta grâce à retourner vers Toi. J'étais comme mort, Tu m'as ranimé par l'eau de la vie. J'étais desséché, Tu m'as ressuscité par le flot céleste de ta parole qui s'est écoulé de la Plume du Très-Miséricordieux.

Ô divine Providence ! Toute existence émane de ta bonté; ne la prive pas des eaux de ta générosité et ne l'éloigne pas de l'océan de ta miséricorde. Je Te supplie de m'aider et de me secourir en tout temps et en toutes circonstances, et je demande, au ciel de ta grâce, ton antique faveur.

Tu es, en vérité, le Seigneur généreux et le Souverain du royaume de l'éternité.

—BAHÁ'U'LLÁH

Drawing Sustenance from God

Derivando Sustento de Dios

Trouver sa subsistance en Dieu

O my Lord! Make Thy beauty to be my food, and Thy presence my drink, and Thy pleasure my hope, and praise of Thee my action, and remembrance of Thee my companion, and the power of Thy sovereignty my succorer, and Thy habitation my home, and my dwelling-place the seat Thou hast sanctified from the limitations imposed upon them who are shut out as by a veil from Thee.

Thou art, verily, the Almighty, the All-Glorious, the Most Powerful.

—BAHÁ'U'LLÁH

¡Oh mi Señor! Haz de tu belleza mi alimento y de tu presencia mi bebida, de tu agrado mi esperanza y de tu alabanza mi acción, de tu recuerdo mi compañero y del poder de tu soberanía mi socorro, de tu morada mi hogar y de mi vivienda, la sede que Tú has santificado de las limitaciones impuestas a quienes están separados de Ti como por un velo.

Tú eres, verdaderamente, el Todopoderoso, el Todo Glorioso, el Omnipotente.

—BAHÁ'U'LLÁH

Ô mon Seigneur ! Fais de ta beauté ma nourriture, de ta présence mon breuvage, de ton plaisir mon espoir, de ta louange mon action, de ton souvenir mon compagnon, de ta puissance souveraine mon secours, de ton habitation mon foyer, et fais que ma demeure soit le lieu que tu as purifié des limitations imposées à ceux qu'un voile sépare de toi.

Tu es en vérité le Tout-Puissant, l'infiniment Glorieux, l'Omnipotent.

—BAHÁ'U'LLÁH

SEEKING REUNION WITH GOD

BUSCANDO LA REUNIÓN CON DIOS

RECHERCHER LA RÉUNION AVEC DIEU

From the sweet-scented streams of Thine eternity give me to drink, O my God, and of the fruits of the tree of Thy being enable me to taste, O my Hope! From the crystal springs of Thy love suffer me to quaff, O my Glory, and beneath the shadow of Thine everlasting providence let me abide, O my Light! Within the meadows of Thy nearness, before Thy presence, make me able to roam, O my Beloved, and at the right hand of the throne of Thy mercy, seat me, O my Desire! From the fragrant breezes of Thy joy let a breath pass over me, O my Goal, and into the heights of the paradise of Thy reality let me gain admission, O my Adored One! To the melodies of the dove of Thy oneness suffer me to hearken, O Resplendent One, and through the spirit of Thy power and Thy might quicken me, O my Provider! In the spirit of Thy love keep me steadfast, O my Succorer, and in the path of Thy good pleasure set firm my steps, O my Maker! Within the garden of Thine immortality, before Thy countenance, let me abide for ever, O Thou Who art merciful unto me, and upon the seat of Thy glory stablish me, O Thou

¡De las perfumadas corrientes de tu eternidad dame de beber, oh mi Dios, y de los frutos del árbol de tu ser déjame gustar, oh mi Esperanza! ¡De los manantiales cristalinos de tu amor permíteme beber, oh mi Gloria, y bajo la sombra de tu eterna providencia déjame habitar, oh mi Luz! ¡Dentro de las praderas de tu proximidad, ante tu presencia, haz posible que pueda vagar, oh mi Amado, y a la diestra del trono de tu merced hazme sentar, oh mi Deseo! ¡De las fragantes brisas de tu alegría deja que un soplo llegue hasta mí, oh mi Objetivo, y en las alturas del paraíso de tu realidad permíteme entrar, oh mi Adorado! ¡Las melodías de la paloma de tu unidad permíteme escuchar, oh Tú el Resplandeciente, y mediante el espíritu de tu fuerza y tu poder, vivifícame, oh mi Proveedor! ¡En el espíritu de tu amor mantenme firme, oh mi Auxiliador, y en el sendero de tu complacencia afirma mis pasos, oh mi Hacedor! ¡Dentro del jardín de tu inmortalidad, ante tu semblante, permíteme eternamente habitar, oh Tú Quien eres misericordioso conmigo, y sobre la sede de tu gloria establéceme, oh Tú Quien eres mi poseedor!

Aux flots parfumés de ton éternité laisse-moi m'abreuver, ô mon Dieu, et aux fruits de l'arbre de ton existence permets-moi de goûter, ô mon Espoir.

Aux sources cristallines de ton amour, permets que j'apaise ma soif, ô ma Gloire, et sous l'ombre de ton éternelle providence, laisse-moi demeurer, ô ma Lumière !

Dans les prairies de ton approche, en ta présence, laisse-moi circuler, ô mon Bien-Aimé et à la droite du trône de ta miséricorde, laisse-moi siéger, ô mon Désir.

Qu'un souffle des brises embaumées de ta joie passe sur moi, ô But de ma vie, et qu'au paradis suprême de ta réalité je trouve accès, ô mon Adoré !

Laisse-moi écouter la mélodie chantée par la colombe de ton unité, ô toi le Resplendissant, et par l'esprit de ton pouvoir et de ta puissance, vivifie-moi, ô toi mon bienfaiteur !

Que je reste constant dans l'esprit de ton amour, ô mon Soutien, et que mes pas soient affermis dans le sentier de ton bon plaisir, ô mon Créateur !

Dans le jardin de ton immortalité, en ta présence, laisse-moi demeurer à jamais, ô toi qui es

Who art my Possessor! To the heaven of Thy loving-kindness lift me up, O my Quickener, and unto the Daystar of Thy guidance lead me, O Thou my Attractor! Before the revelations of Thine invisible spirit summon me to be present, O Thou Who art my Origin and my Highest Wish, and unto the essence of the fragrance of Thy beauty, which Thou wilt manifest, cause me to return, O Thou Who art my God!

Potent art Thou to do what pleaseth Thee. Thou art, verily, the Most Exalted, the All-Glorious, the All-Highest.

—BAHÁ'U'LLÁH

¡Hacia el cielo de tu cariñosa bondad elévame, oh mi
Vivificador, y hacia el Sol de tu guía condúceme,
oh Tú mi Atraedor! ¡Ante las revelaciones de tu
invisible espíritu llámame a estar presente, Tú Quien
eres me Origen y mi Elevadísimo Deseo, y hacia la
esencia de la fragrancia de tu belleza, que Tú has de
manifestar, hazme volver, oh Tú Quien eres mi Dios!

Potente eres Tú para hacer lo que Te place.
Tú eres, en verdad, el Más Exaltado, el Todo Glorioso,
el Altísimo.

—BAHÁ'U'LLÁH

miséricordieux pour moi, et sur le siège de ta gloire
établis-moi, ô toi qui es mon maître !

Au ciel de ta tendre bonté élève-moi, ô toi mon
Animateur, et vers l'Étoile matinale de ta direction
conduis-moi, ô toi qui m'attires.

Lors des révélations de ton invisible esprit daigne
m'appeler, ô toi qui es la cause de mon existence et
l'objet de mon plus grand désir, et vers l'essence
embaumée de ta beauté que tu voudras manifester,
fais que je retourne, ô toi qui es mon Dieu !

Tu as le pouvoir de faire ce qui te plaît. Tu es en
vérité le Très-Élevé, le Tout-Glorieux, le Suprême.

—BAHÁ'U'LLÁH

SUPPLICATING SPIRITUAL ENRICHMENT

SUPLICANDO ENRIQUECIMIENTO ESPIRITUAL

SUPPLIER POUR OBTENIR L'ENRICHISSEMENT SPIRITUEL

O God, Who art the Author of all Manifestations, the Source of all Sources, the Fountainhead of all Revelations, and the Wellspring of all Lights! I testify that by Thy Name the heaven of understanding hath been adorned, and the ocean of utterance hath surged, and the dispensations of Thy providence have been promulgated unto the followers of all religions.

I beseech Thee so to enrich me as to dispense with all save Thee, and be made independent of anyone except Thyself. Rain down, then, upon me out of the clouds of Thy bounty that which shall profit me in every world of Thy worlds. Assist me, then, through Thy strengthening grace, so to serve Thy Cause amidst Thy servants that I may show forth what will cause me to be remembered as long as Thine own kingdom endureth and Thy dominion will last.

This is Thy servant, O my Lord, who with his whole being hath turned unto the horizon of Thy bounty, and the ocean of Thy grace, and the heaven of Thy gifts. Do with me then as becometh Thy majesty, and Thy glory, and Thy bounteousness, and Thy grace.

¡Oh Dios, Quien eres el Autor de todas las Manifestaciones, el Origen de todos los Orígenes, la Fuente Suprema de toda Revelación, y el Manantial de toda Luz! Atestiguo que, por tu Nombre, el cielo de la comprensión ha sido adornado y el océano de la prolación se ha agitado, y las dispensaciones de tu providencia han sido promulgadas a los seguidores de toda religión.

Yo Te imploro, que me enriquezcas a tal punto que pueda prescindir de todo salvo de Ti, y no depender de nadie excepto de Ti.

Derrama, entonces, sobre mí, de las nubes de tu bondad, aquello que me beneficie en cada mundo de tus mundos. Ayúdame, entonces, mediante tu gracia fortalecedora, a servir de tal modo a tu Causa entre tus siervos, que pueda demostrar aquello que me haga ser recordado tanto como perdure tu propio reino y persista tu dominio.

Oh mi Señor, este es tu siervo que se ha vuelto con todo su ser hacia el horizonte de tu munificencia, el océano de tu gracia, y el cielo de tus dádivas. Procede conmigo como corresponde a tu majestad, a tu gloria, a tu generosidad, y a tu gracia.

Ô Dieu qui est l'Auteur de toutes les manifestations, la Source de toutes les sources, l'Origine de toutes les révélations et de toutes les lumières! J'atteste que ton nom a été l'ornement du ciel de la connaissance, que par ton nom a surgi l'océan de la parole et que par lui, pour les fidèles de toutes les religions, ont été promulguées les dispensations de ta providence.

Je te supplie de m'enrichir au point que je puisse me dispenser de tout et devenir indépendant de tous, sauf de toi-même. Des nuées de ta générosité, fais descendre sur moi ce qui me sera profitable en chacun de tes mondes. Aide-moi par ta grâce fortifiante à servir si bien ta cause parmi tes serviteurs, que je puisse manifester ce qui perpétuera mon souvenir aussi longtemps que dureront ton royaume et ta souveraineté.

Voici ton serviteur, ô mon Seigneur qui, de tout son être, s'est tourné vers l'horizon de ta générosité, l'océan de ta grâce et le ciel de tes dons. Agis envers moi comme il sied à ta majesté, à ta gloire, à ta générosité et à ta grâce.

Thou, in truth, art the God of strength and power,
Who art meet to answer them that pray Thee.
There is no God save Thee, the All-Knowing, the
All-Wise.

—BAHÁ'U'LLÁH

Tú eres, en verdad, el Dios de fuerza y poder,
Quien es capaz de contestar a aquellos que Le invocan.
No hay Dios sino Tú, el Omnisciente, el Sapientísimo.

—BAHÁ'U'LLÁH

Tu es en vérité le Dieu de force et de puissance.
Tu as le pouvoir d'exaucer ceux qui te prient. Il n'y a
pas d'autre dieu que toi, l'Omniscient, l'infiniment
Sage.

—BAHÁ'U'LLÁH

INVOKING THE POWER TO TEACH

INVOCANDO EL PODER DE ENSEÑAR

INVOQUER LE POUVOIR DE L'ENSEIGNEMENT

Praise be to Thee, O Lord my God! I implore Thee, by Thy Name which none hath befittingly recognized, and whose import no soul hath fathomed; I beseech Thee, by Him Who is the Fountainhead of Thy Revelation and the Dayspring of Thy signs, to make my heart to be a receptacle of Thy love and of remembrance of Thee. Knit it, then, to Thy most great Ocean, that from it may flow out the living waters of Thy wisdom and the crystal streams of Thy glorification and praise.

The limbs of my body testify to Thy unity, and the hair of my head declareth the power of Thy sovereignty and might. I have stood at the door of Thy grace with utter self-effacement and complete abnegation, and clung to the hem of Thy bounty, and fixed mine eyes upon the horizon of Thy gifts.

Do Thou destine for me, O my God, what becometh the greatness of Thy majesty, and assist me, by Thy strengthening grace, so to teach Thy Cause that the dead may speed out of their sepulchers,

¡Alabado seas, oh Señor mi Dios! Te imploro por tu Nombre, el cual nadie ha reconocido dignamente y cuya significación ningún alma ha podido sondear, y Te suplico por Aquel Quien es la Fuente de tu Revelación y la Aurora de tus signos, que hagas de mi corazón un receptáculo de tu amor y de tu recuerdo. Únelo, entonces, a tu más grande océano, para que de él emanen las aguas vivientes de tu sabiduría y los torrentes cristalinos de tu glorificación y alabanza.

Los miembros de mi cuerpo testifican tu unidad y el pelo de mi cabeza declara la fuerza de tu soberanía y poder. He permanecido ante la puerta de tu gracia con absoluta humildad y completa abnegación y me he asido al borde de tu munificencia y he fijado mis ojos en el horizonte de tus dádivas.

Destina para mí, oh mi Dios, lo que convenga a la grandeza de tu majestad, y ayúdame con tu gracia fotalecedora a enseñar tu Causa, de modo tal que los muertos salgan de sus tumbas y se precipiten hacia Ti,

Loué sois-tu, ô Seigneur mon Dieu ! Je t'implore par ton nom, que nul n'a reconnu pleinement et dont aucune âme n'a sondé l'importance, je te supplie par la Source de ta révélation et l'Aurore de tes signes, de faire de mon cœur le réceptacle de ton amour et de ton souvenir. Unis-le donc à ton Océan infini, afin que de lui puissent ruisseler les eaux vives de ta sagesse et les flots cristallins de ta glorification et de ta louange.

Les membres de mon corps attestent ton unité, et les cheveux de ma tête proclament la force de ton pouvoir souverain. Je me tiens sur le seuil de ta grâce dans l'humilité et le renoncement les plus complets. J'ai saisi le pan de ta robe de miséricorde et j'ai fixé mon regard sur l'horizon de tes dons.

Accorde-moi, ô mon Dieu, ce qui convient à la grandeur de ta majesté et aide-moi, par ta grâce fortifiante, à enseigner ta cause de telle sorte que les morts surgissent de leurs sépulcres et qu'ils s'élancent

and rush forth towards Thee, trusting wholly in Thee,
and fixing their gaze upon the orient of Thy Cause,
and the dawning-place of Thy Revelation.

  Thou, verily, art the Most Powerful,
the Most High, the All-Knowing, the All-Wise.

—*BAHÁ'U'LLÁH*

confiando plenamente en Ti y fijando su mirada en el oriente de tu Causa y en el punto de amanecer de tu Revelación.

Tú eres, verdaderamente, el Más Poderoso, el Altísimo, el Omnisciente, el Omnisapiente.

—*BAHÁ'U'LLÁH*

vers toi, pleins de confiance en toi, les regards fixés sur l'Orient de ta cause et l'Aurore de ta révélation.

Tu es, en vérité, le Puissant, le Très-Haut, l'Omniscient, le Sage.

—*BAHÁ'U'LLÁH*

SEEKING RECEPTIVE SOULS

BUSCANDO ALMAS RECEPTIVAS

RECHERCHER LES ÂMES RECEPTIVES

All praise, O my God, be to Thee Who art the Source of all glory and majesty, of greatness and honor, of sovereignty and dominion, of loftiness and grace, of awe and power. Whomsoever Thou willest Thou causest to draw nigh unto the Most Great Ocean, and on whomsoever Thou desirest Thou conferrest the honor of recognizing Thy Most Ancient Name. Of all who are in heaven and on earth, none can withstand the operation of Thy sovereign Will. From all eternity Thou didst rule the entire creation, and Thou wilt continue for evermore to exercise Thy dominion over all created things. There is none other God but Thee, the Almighty, the Most Exalted, the All-Powerful, the All-Wise.

Illumine, O Lord, the faces of Thy servants, that they may behold Thee; and cleanse their hearts that they may turn unto the court of Thy heavenly favors, and recognize Him Who is the Manifestation of Thy Self and the Dayspring of Thine Essence. Verily, Thou art the Lord of all worlds. There is no God but Thee, the Unconstrained, the All-Subduing.

—BAHÁ'U'LLÁH

Toda alabanza sea para Ti, oh mi Dios, Quien eres la Fuente de toda gloria y majestad, de grandeza y honor, de soberanía y dominio, de sublimidad y gracia, de reverencia y poder. De acuerdo con tu voluntad, Tú haces acercarse al Más Grande Océano a quien Tú deseas y le confieres el honor de reconocer tu Muy Antiguo Nombre. De todos los que están en el cielo y en la tierra, nadie puede resistir la acción de tu soberana Voluntad. Desde toda la eternidad Tú registe la creación entera, y continuarás siempre ejerciendo tu dominio sobre todo lo creado. No hay otro Dios más que Tú, el Omnipotente, el Exaltadísimo, el Todopoderoso, el Sapientísimo.

Ilumina, oh Señor, los rostros de tus siervos, para que ellos puedan verte; purifica sus corazones para que puedan volverse hacia la corte de tus divinos favores, y reconocer a Aquel Quien es la Manifestación de tu Ser y la Aurora de tu Esencia. Verdaderamente, Tú eres el Señor de todos los mundos. No hay Dios sino Tú, el Libre, el que Todo lo Domina.

—BAHÁ'U'LLÁH

Toutes louanges, ô mon Dieu, soient à toi qui es la Source de toute gloire et majesté, de grandeur et d'honneur, de souveraineté et d'empire, d'élévation et de grâce, de crainte et de puissance. Tu diriges qui tu veux vers ton très grand Océan, et à qui bon te semble, tu confères l'honneur de reconnaître ton très ancien nom. De tous ceux qui sont au ciel et sur terre, aucun ne peut résister à l'action de ta volonté souveraine. De toute éternité tu gouvernas la création tout entière et tu continueras à jamais à exercer ton empire sur toutes choses créées. Il n'est point d'autre dieu que toi, le Tout-Puissant, le Glorifié, l'Omnipotent, l'infiniment Sage.

Éclaire, ô Seigneur, le visage de tes serviteurs afin qu'ils puissent te contempler; purifie leur cœur pour qu'ils se tournent vers le parvis de tes faveurs célestes et qu'ils reconnaissent celui qui est la manifestation de toi-même et l'Aurore de ton essence.

En vérité tu es le Seigneur de tous les mondes. Il n'est pas d'autre dieu que toi, l'Invincible, le Victorieux.

—BAHÁ'U'LLÁH

INVOKING STEADFASTNESS IN GOD'S
COMMANDMENTS

INVOCANDO LA CONSTANCIA ANTE LOS
MANDAMIENTOS DIVINOS

DEMANDER LA FERMETÉ DANS LES COMMANDEMENTS
DE DIEU

O my God! O my God! Unite the hearts of Thy servants, and reveal to them Thy great purpose. May they follow Thy commandments and abide in Thy law. Help them, O God, in their endeavor, and grant them strength to serve Thee. O God! Leave them not to themselves, but guide their steps by the light of Thy knowledge, and cheer their hearts by Thy love. Verily, Thou art their Helper and their Lord.

—BAHÁ'U'LLÁH

¡Oh mi Dios! ¡Oh mi Dios! Une los corazones de tus siervos y revélales tu gran propósito. Puedan ellos seguir tus mandamientos y atenerse a tu ley. Ayúdales, oh Dios, en sus esfuerzos y confiéreles fuerza para servirte. ¡Oh Dios! No los abandones a sí mismos, sino guía sus pasos con la luz de tu conocimiento y anima sus corazones con tu amor. Verdaderamente, Tú eres su Ayuda y su Señor.

—*BAHÁ'U'LLÁH*

Ô mon Dieu ! Ô mon Dieu !
Unis les cœurs de tes serviteurs et révèle-leur ton grand dessein. Puissent-ils suivre tes commandements et observer ta loi ! Aide-les, ô mon Dieu, dans leurs efforts et accorde-leur la force de te servir.

Ô Dieu, ne les abandonne pas à eux-mêmes mais, par la lumière de ta connaissance, guide leurs pas, et par ton amour réjouis leur cœur.

En vérité, tu es leur Recours et leur Seigneur.

—*BAHÁ'U'LLÁH*

ENTREATING THE STRENGTH OF GOD

SUPLICANDO LA FUERZA DE DIOS

SUPPLIER LA FORCE DE DIEU

Lauded be Thy Name, O Lord my God! I am Thy servant who hath laid hold on the cord of Thy tender mercies, and clung to the hem of Thy bounteousness. I entreat Thee by Thy name whereby Thou hast subjected all created things, both visible and invisible, and through which the breath that is life indeed was wafted over the entire creation, to strengthen me by Thy power which hath encompassed the heavens and the earth, and to guard me from all sickness and tribulation. I bear witness that Thou art the Lord of all names, and the Ordainer of all that may please Thee. There is none other God but Thee, the Almighty, the All-Knowing, the All-Wise.

Do Thou ordain for me, O my Lord, what will profit me in every world of Thy worlds. Supply me, then, with what Thou hast written down for the chosen ones among Thy creatures, whom neither the blame of the blamer, nor the clamor of the infidel, nor the estrangement of such as have withdrawn from Thee, hath deterred from turning towards Thee.

Thou, truly, art the Help in Peril through the power of Thy sovereignty. No God is there save Thee, the Almighty, the Most Powerful.

—BAHÁ'U'LLÁH

¡Loado sea tu Nombre, oh Señor mi Dios! Soy tu siervo que se ha asido al cordón de tu tierna misericordia y aferrado al borde de tu benevolencia. Te suplico por tu nombre, mediante el cual Tú has sometido a todas las cosas creadas, visibles e invisibles, y por el cual el hálito que es verdadera vida ha sido difundido sobre toda la creación, que me fortalezcas con tu poder que envuelve los cielos y la tierra, y me libres de toda enfermedad y tribulación. Atestiguo que Tú eres el Señor de todos los nombres, y ordenas todo lo que Te place. No hay otro Dios sino Tú, el Todopoderoso, el Omnisciente, el Sapientísimo.

Ordena para mí, oh mi Señor, lo que me beneficie en cada mundo de tus mundos. Provéeme, pues, con lo que Tú has destinado para los elegidos entre tus criaturas, a quienes ni la censura del crítico, ni el clamor del infiel, ni el distanciamiento de aquellos que se han alejado de Ti, les han impedido volverse hacia Ti.

Tú, verdaderamente, eres el que Ayuda en el Peligro mediante el poder de tu soberanía. No hay Dios sino Tú, el Todopoderoso, el Omnipotente.

—BAHÁ'U'LLÁH

Loué soit ton nom, ô Seigneur mon Dieu ! Je suis ton serviteur qui s'accroche à la corde de tes tendres miséricordes et qui se retient à la frange de ta munificence ! Je te supplie, par ton nom qui a soumis toutes choses, tant visibles qu'invisibles, et par lequel le souffle de la vraie vie s'est répandu sur toute la création, de me fortifier par ton pouvoir qui s'est étendu sur la terre et le ciel, et de me garder de toute maladie et tribulation. J'atteste que tu es le Seigneur de tous les noms et l'Ordonnateur de tout ce qui est conforme à ton bon plaisir. Il n'y a pas d'autre dieu que toi, le Tout-Puissant, l'Informé, le Sage.

Ordonne pour moi, ô mon Seigneur, ce qui me sera profitable en chacun de tes mondes. Donne-moi donc ce que tu as promis à tes créatures élues, que ni le blâme de l'accusateur, ni les clameurs de l'infidèle, ni l'aliénation du cœur de ceux qui se sont éloignés de toi n'ont empêché de se tourner vers toi.

En vérité, tu es l'Aide dans le péril, par la puissance de ta souveraineté. Il n'y a pas d'autre dieu que toi, le Très-Haut, le Tout-Puissant.

—BAHÁ'U'LLÁH

Beseeching God's Grace and Mercy

Rogando por la Gracia y Misericordia de Dios

Implorer la grâce et la miséricorde de Dieu

My God, Whom I worship and adore! I bear witness unto Thy unity and Thy oneness, and acknowledge Thy gifts, both in the past and in the present. Thou art the All-Bountiful, the overflowing showers of Whose mercy have rained down upon high and low alike, and the splendors of Whose grace have been shed over both the obedient and the rebellious.

O God of mercy, before Whose door the quintessence of mercy hath bowed down, and round the sanctuary of Whose Cause loving-kindness, in its inmost spirit, hath circled, we beseech Thee, entreating Thine ancient grace, and seeking Thy present favor, that Thou mayest have mercy upon all who are the manifestations of the world of being, and deny them not the outpourings of Thy grace in Thy days.

All are but poor and needy, and Thou, verily, art the All-Possessing, the All-Subduing, the All-Powerful.

—BAHÁ'U'LLÁH

¡Mi Dios, a Quien venero y adoro! Soy testigo de tu unidad y tu unicidad, y reconozco tus dádivas, del pasado y del presente. Tú eres el Todo Generoso, y las anegantes lluvias de tu misericordia se han vertido sobre pobres y ricos, y los esplendores de tu gracia se han derramado sobre los obedientes y los rebeldes.

Oh Dios de Misericordia, ante cuya puerta se ha inclinado la quintaesencia de la misericordia y alrededor del santuario de cuya Causa ha circundado la cariñosa bondad en su más íntimo espíritu, Te suplicamos rogando a tu antigua gracia y anhelando tu presente favor, que tengas piedad de todos los que son las manifestaciones del mundo del ser y no les niegues la efusión de tu gracia en tus días.

Todos son pobres y necesitados, y Tú, verdaderamente, eres el que Todo lo Posee, el que Todo lo Domina, el Omnipotente.

—BAHÁ'U'LLÁH

Mon Dieu, que je vénère et que j'adore ! J'atteste ton unité et ton unicité ; je reconnais tes dons, passés et présents. Tu es le Généreux ! Les flots débordants de ta merci se sont déversés sur les petits comme sur les grands, et les splendeurs de ta grâce se sont répandues sur le rebelle aussi bien que sur l'homme docile.

Ô Dieu de merci ! La quintessence de la miséricorde s'est inclinée devant ta porte, et l'esprit d'amour, au plus profond de lui-même, a tourné autour du tabernacle de ta cause ; nous te supplions, en faisant appel à ta grâce passée et en sollicitant tes présentes faveurs, d'avoir pitié de tous ceux qui sont des manifestations du monde de l'existence et de ne point leur refuser l'abondance de ta grâce, en tes jours.

Nous ne sommes que des pauvres et des nécessiteux, et toi, en vérité, tu es le Possesseur et le Maître de toutes choses, le Tout-Puissant.

—BAHÁ'U'LLÁH

IMPLORING THE BESTOWALS OF GOD

IMPLORANDO LOS DONES DIVINOS

SOLLICITER LES DONS DE DIEU

Glorified art Thou, O Lord my God! I implore Thee by the onrushing winds of Thy grace, and by them Who are the Daysprings of Thy purpose and the Dawning-Places of Thine inspiration, to send down upon me and upon all that have sought Thy face that which beseemeth Thy generosity and bountiful grace, and is worthy of Thy bestowals and favors. Poor and desolate I am, O my Lord! Immerse me in the ocean of Thy wealth; athirst, suffer me to drink from the living waters of Thy loving-kindness.

I beseech Thee, by Thine own Self and by Him Whom Thou hast appointed as the Manifestation of Thine own Being and Thy discriminating Word unto all that are in heaven and on earth, to gather together Thy servants beneath the shade of the Tree of Thy gracious providence. Help them, then, to partake of its fruits, to incline their ears to the rustling of its leaves, and to the sweetness of the voice of the Bird that chanteth upon its branches. Thou art, verily, the Help in Peril, the Inaccessible, the Almighty, the Most Bountiful.

—BAHÁ'U'LLÁH

¡Glorificado eres Tú, oh Señor mi Dios! Te imploro, por los impetuosos vientos de tu gracia, y por Aquellos que son las Auroras de tu propósito y los Puntos de Amanecer de tu inspiración, que me envíes a mí y a todos aquellos que han buscado tu rostro, lo que corresponda a tu generosidad y munífica gracia y sea digno de tus dádivas y favores. ¡Estoy pobre y desolado, oh mi Señor! Sumérgeme en el océano de tu riqueza; estoy sediento, permíteme beber de las aguas vivientes de tu cariñosa bondad.

Te suplico, por tu propia Esencia, y por Aquel a Quien Tú designaste como la Manifestación de tu propio Ser y tu Palabra discriminatoria para todos los que están en el cielo y la tierra, que reúnas a tus siervos a la sombra del Árbol de tu bondadosa providencia. Ayúdales, entonces, a compartir sus frutos, a inclinar sus oídos hacia el murmullo de sus hojas y hacia la dulzura de la voz del Ave que canta sobre sus ramas. Tú eres, verdaderamente, el que Ayuda en el Peligro, el Inaccesible, el Todopoderoso, el Más Generoso.

—BAHÁ'U'LLÁH

Glorifié es-tu, ô Seigneur mon Dieu ! Je t'implore par les souffles impétueux de ta grâce et par les Aurores de ton dessein et les Aubes de ton inspiration, de faire descendre sur moi et sur tous ceux qui ont voulu contempler ta face ce qui convient à la surabondance de ta munificence et de tes bienfaits. Me voici pauvre et désolé, ô mon Seigneur ! Plonge-moi dans l'océan de tes richesses; je suis accablé par la soif, permets que je me désaltère des eaux vives de ta tendre bonté.

Je te supplie, par toi-même et par celui que tu as choisi pour être la Manifestation de toi-même et ton Verbe qui a le pouvoir de juger les habitants de la terre et du ciel, de rassembler tes serviteurs à l'ombre de l'Arbre de ta munificente providence. Aide-les donc à recevoir leur part de ses fruits, à tendre une oreille attentive au bruissement de ses feuilles et à la douce voix de l'Oiseau qui chantait sur ses branches. Tu es, en vérité, le Secours dans le péril, l'Inaccessible, le Tout-Puissant, le Plus Généreux.

—BAHÁ'U'LLÁH

ENTREATING GOD'S GENEROSITY

ROGANDO POR LA GENEROSIDAD DE DIOS

PRIER POUR LA GÉNÉROSITÉ DE DIEU

O Thou Whose face is the object of my adoration, Whose beauty is my sanctuary, Whose habitation is my goal, Whose praise is my hope, Whose providence is my companion, Whose love is the cause of my being, Whose mention is my solace, Whose nearness is my desire, Whose presence is my dearest wish and highest aspiration, I entreat Thee not to withhold from me the things Thou didst ordain for the chosen ones among Thy servants. Supply me, then, with the good of this world and of the next.

Thou, truly, art the King of all men. There is no God but Thee, the Ever-Forgiving, the Most Generous.

—BAHÁ'U'LLÁH

Oh Tú cuyo rostro es el objeto de mi adoración, cuya belleza es mi santuario, cuya morada es mi objetivo, cuya alabanza es mi esperanza, cuya providencia es mi compañera, cuyo amor es la causa de mi existencia, cuya mención es mi consuelo, cuya proximidad es mi deseo, cuya presencia es mi más caro anhelo y elevadísima aspiración; Te suplico que no me niegues aquello que Tú ordenaste para los elegidos entre tus siervos. Provéeme, entonces, con el bien de este mundo y del venidero.

Tú, verdaderamente, eres el Rey de todos los hombres. No hay Dios sino Tú, el Siempre Perdonador, el Más Generoso.

—BAHÁ'U'LLÁH

Ô toi dont le visage est l'objet de mon adoration, la beauté est mon sanctuaire et le domaine mon but, dont la louange est mon espoir et la providence ma compagne, dont l'amour est la cause de mon existence, la mention ma consolation, l'approche mon désir, la présence mon vœu le plus cher et ma plus haute aspiration, je te prie de ne pas me refuser ce que tu as ordonné pour les élus parmi tes serviteurs. Accorde-moi donc les bienfaits de ce monde et de l'autre.

Tu es, en vérité, le Roi de tous les hommes. Il n'est point d'autre dieu que toi, celui qui toujours pardonne, le Très-Généreux.

—BAHÁ'U'LLÁH

SUPPLICATING GOD'S STRENGTH AND HEALING

SUPLICANDO LA CURACIÓN Y FUERZA DIVINA

SUPPLIER LA FORCE ET LA GUÉRISON DE DIEU

O God, my God! I beg of Thee by the ocean of Thy healing, and by the splendors of the Daystar of Thy grace, and by Thy Name through which Thou didst subdue Thy servants, and by the pervasive power of Thy most exalted Word and the potency of Thy most august Pen, and by Thy mercy that hath preceded the creation of all who are in heaven and on earth, to purge me with the waters of Thy bounty from every affliction and disorder, and from all weakness and feebleness.

Thou seest, O my Lord, Thy suppliant waiting at the door of Thy bounty, and him who hath set his hopes on Thee clinging to the cord of Thy generosity. Deny him not, I beseech Thee, the things he seeketh from the ocean of Thy grace and the Daystar of Thy loving-kindness.

Powerful art Thou to do what pleaseth Thee. There is none other God save Thee, the Ever-Forgiving, the Most Generous.

—BAHÁ'U'LLÁH

¡Oh Dios, mi Dios! Yo Te pido por el océano de tu curación y por el resplandor del Sol de tu gracia, y por tu Nombre por el cual sometiste a tus siervos, y por el poder penetrante de tu muy exaltada Palabra, y la potencia de tu muy augusta Pluma, y por tu misericordia que ha precedido la creación de todos los que están en el cielo y en la tierra, me purifiques con las aguas de tu generosidad de toda aflicción y dolencia y de toda debilidad y flaqueza.

Tú ves, oh mi Señor, a tu suplicante, esperando a la puerta de tu munificencia, y a quien ha puesto sus esperanzas en Ti, aferrándose al cordón de tu generosidad. Te suplico, no le niegues aquello que solicita del océano de tu gracia y del Sol de tu amorosa bondad.

Poderoso eres Tú para hacer lo que Te place. No hay otro Dios sino Tú, el Siempre Perdonador, el más Generoso.

—BAHÁ'U'LLÁH

Ô Dieu, mon Dieu ! Je te demande, par l'océan de ta guérison, par les splendeurs de l'étoile matinale de ta grâce par ton nom qui a conquis tes serviteurs, par le pouvoir persuasif de ta parole très exaltée, par la puissance de ta plume très auguste, et par ta miséricorde qui a précédé la création de tout ce qui existe au ciel et sur la terre, de me purifier par les eaux de ta bonté, de toute affliction et désordre, de toute faiblesse et débilité.

Tu vois, ô mon Seigneur, ton serviteur suppliant à la porte de ta bonté et qui, accroché à la corde de ta générosité, a placé son espoir en toi. Ne lui refuse pas, je t'en supplie, ce qu'il sollicite de l'Océan de ta grâce et de l'Étoile du matin de ta tendre bonté.

Tu as le pouvoir de faire ce qui te plaît. Il n'est pas d'autre dieu que toi, celui qui sans cesse pardonne, le Très-Généreux.

—BAHÁ'U'LLÁH

IMPLORING SPIRITUAL CONSTANCY

IMPLORANDO LA CONSTANCIA ESPIRITUAL

IMPLORER LA CONSTANCE SPIRITUELLE

Magnified be Thy name, O Lord my God! Thou art He Whom all things worship and Who worshipeth no one, Who is the Lord of all things and is the vassal of none, Who knoweth all things and is known of none. Thou didst wish to make Thyself known unto men; therefore, Thou didst, through a word of Thy mouth, bring creation into being and fashion the universe. There is none other God except Thee, the Fashioner, the Creator, the Almighty, the Most Powerful.

I implore Thee, by this very word that hath shone forth above the horizon of Thy will, to enable me to drink deep of the living waters through which Thou hast vivified the hearts of Thy chosen ones and quickened the souls of them that love Thee, that I may, at all times and under all conditions, turn my face wholly towards Thee.

Thou art the God of power, of glory and bounty. No God is there beside Thee, the Supreme Ruler, the All-Glorious, the Omniscient.

—BAHÁ'U'LLÁH

¡Magnificado sea tu Nombre, oh Señor mi Dios! Tú eres Aquel a Quien todo adora y no adora a nadie, Quien es el Señor de todo y no es vasallo de nadie, Quien todo lo conoce y no es conocido de nadie. Tú quisiste que los hombres Te conocieran; por tanto, mediante una palabra de tu boca formaste la creación y modelaste el universo. No hay Dios sino Tú, el Modelador, el Creador, el Todopoderoso, el Omnipotente.

Te imploro, por esta misma palabra que ha brillado sobre el horizonte de tu voluntad, me permitas beber abundantemente de las aguas de vida con que Tú has vivificado los corazones de tus elegidos y hecho revivir las almas de aquellos que Te aman, para que pueda en todo momento y en toda condición, volver mi rostro completamente hacia Ti.

Tú eres el Dios de poder, de gloria y munificencia. No hay Dios sino Tú, el Gobernante Supremo, el Todo Glorioso, el Omnisciente.

—BAHÁ'U'LLÁH

Magnifié soit ton nom, ô Seigneur mon Dieu ! Tu es celui que toutes choses adorent et qui n'en adore aucune, qui est le Seigneur de toutes choses et n'est le vassal d'aucune. Tu as la connaissance de toutes choses et n'es connu d'aucune. Tu voulus te faire connaître des hommes, c'est pourquoi, par un mot de ta bouche, tu amenas le monde à l'existence et façonnas l'univers. Il n'y a pas d'autre dieu que toi, le Façonneur, le Créateur, le Très-Haut, le Tout-Puissant.

Je t'implore, par cette parole même qui a brillé à l'horizon de ta volonté, de permettre que je m'abreuve des eaux vives par lesquelles tu as vivifié les cœurs de tes élus et ranimé les âmes de ceux qui t'aiment, afin que je puisse en tout temps et en toute circonstance, diriger uniquement vers toi mon visage.

Tu es le Dieu de la puissance, de la gloire et de la munificence. Il n'y a pas d'autre dieu que toi, l'Ordonnateur suprême, le Glorieux, l'Omniscient.

—BAHÁ'U'LLÁH

APPEALING FOR SPIRITUAL TRANSFORMATION

ROGANDO POR LA TRANSFORMACIÓN ESPIRITUAL

CONJURER LA TRANSFORMATION SPIRITUELLE

Create in me a pure heart, O my God, and renew a tranquil conscience within me, O my Hope! Through the spirit of power confirm Thou me in Thy Cause, O my Best-Beloved, and by the light of Thy glory reveal unto me Thy path, O Thou the Goal of my desire! Through the power of Thy transcendent might lift me up unto the heaven of Thy holiness, O Source of my being, and by the breezes of Thine eternity gladden me, O Thou Who art my God! Let Thine everlasting melodies breathe tranquillity on me, O my Companion, and let the riches of Thine ancient countenance deliver me from all except Thee, O my Master, and let the tidings of the revelation of Thine incorruptible Essence bring me joy, O Thou Who art the most manifest of the manifest and the most hidden of the hidden!

—BAHÁ'U'LLÁH

¡Crea en mí un corazón puro, oh mi Dios, y renueva una conciencia tranquila dentro de mí, oh mi Esperanza! ¡Por medio del espíritu del poder, confírmame en tu Causa, oh mi Bienamado, y por la luz de tu gloria, revélame tu sendero, oh Tú el Objeto de mi deseo! ¡Mediante la fuerza de tu trascendente poder, elévame hacia el cielo de tu santidad, oh Fuente de mi ser, y por las brisas de tu eternidad alégrame, oh Tú Quien eres mi Dios! ¡Haz que tus eternas melodías me inspiren tranquilidad, oh mi Compañero y que las riquezas de tu antiguo semblante, me libren de todo excepto de Ti, oh mi Maestro, y que las nuevas de la revelación de tu incorruptible Esencia, me traigan alegría, oh Tú Quien eres lo más manifiesto de lo manifiesto y lo más oculto de lo oculto!

—BAHÁ'U'LLÁH

Crée en moi un cœur pur, ô mon Dieu et renouvelle en moi une conscience paisible, ô mon espérance ! Par l'esprit de puissance, confirme-moi en ta cause, ô mon Bien-Aimé, et que la lumière de ta gloire me révèle ta voie, ô toi, le but de mon désir !

Par la vertu de ton pouvoir transcendant, élève-moi jusqu'au ciel de ta sainteté, ô source de mon être, et par les brises de ton éternité réjouis mon âme, ô toi qui es mon Dieu !

Que tes éternelles mélodies m'apportent la tranquillité, ô mon Compagnon; que les richesses de ton ancien visage me délivrent de tout ce qui n'est pas toi, ô mon Maître, et que les bonnes nouvelles de la révélation de ton incorruptible Essence m'emplissent de joie, ô toi, suprême évidence parmi les manifestés, toi le plus secret des mystères.

—BAHÁ'U'LLÁH

EVENING
COMMITTING ONESELF TO THE WILL OF GOD

NOCHE
DEDICÁNDOSE A LA VOLUNTAD DE DIOS

SOIR
SE SOUMETTRE À LA VOLONTÉ DE DIEU

How can I choose to sleep, O God, my God, when the eyes of them that long for Thee are wakeful because of their separation from Thee; and how can I lie down to rest whilst the souls of Thy lovers are sore vexed in their remoteness from Thy presence?

I have committed, O my Lord, my spirit and my entire being into the right hand of Thy might and Thy protection, and I lay my head on my pillow through Thy power, and lift it up according to Thy will and Thy good pleasure. Thou art, in truth, the Preserver, the Keeper, the Almighty, the Most Powerful.

By Thy might! I ask not, whether sleeping or waking, but that which Thou dost desire. I am Thy servant and in Thy hands. Do Thou graciously aid me to do what will shed forth the fragrance of Thy good pleasure. This, truly, is my hope and the hope of them that enjoy near access to Thee. Praised be Thou, O Lord of the worlds!

—BAHÁ'U'LLÁH

¿Cómo puedo desear dormir, oh Dios, mi Dios, cuando los ojos de aquellos que Te anhelan están despiertos debido a su separación de Ti? ¿Y cómo puedo yo descansar, mientras las almas de quienes Te aman están adoloridas por hallarse alejadas de tu presencia?

Oh mi Señor, he encomendado mi espíritu y todo mi ser a la diestra de tu poder y tu protección, y reposo mi cabeza sobre la almohada por medio de tu poder, y la levanto de acuerdo con tu voluntad y tu complacencia. Tú eres, en verdad, el que Preserva, el Guardián, el Omnipotente, el Poderosísimo.

¡Por tu poder! Yo solo pido, sea dormido o despierto, aquello que Tú deseas. Soy tu siervo y estoy en tus manos. Ayúdame bondadosamente a realizar aquello que pueda derramar la fragancia de tu agrado. Esta es, en verdad, mi esperanza y la esperanza de aquellos que gozan de tu cercanía. ¡Alabado seas, oh Señor de los mundos!

—BAHÁ'U'LLÁH

Comment puis-je préférer le sommeil, ô Dieu, mon Dieu, alors que ceux qui aspirent à toi restent éveillés parce qu'ils sont séparés de toi; et comment puis-je m'étendre pour me reposer pendant que les âmes de ceux qui t'aiment souffrent d'être éloignées de ta présence ?

J'ai remis, ô mon Seigneur, mon esprit et tout mon être dans la main droite de ta puissance et de ta protection; par ton pouvoir, je pose ma tête sur l'oreiller et je la lève selon ta volonté et ton bon plaisir. Tu es en vérité le Protecteur, le Vigilant, le Tout-Puissant, l'Omnipotent.

Par ton pouvoir ! Je ne demande, endormi ou éveillé, que ce que tu désires. Je suis ton serviteur et je suis entre tes mains. Aide-moi généreusement à accomplir ce qu'il faut pour que se répande le parfum de ton bon plaisir. C'est là en vérité mon espoir et l'espoir de ceux qui se plaisent auprès de toi.

Loué sois-tu, ô Seigneur des mondes !

—BAHÁ'U'LLÁH

EVENING
RESTING IN GOD'S CARE AND PROTECTION

NOCHE
AMPARÁNDOSE EN EL CUIDADO Y LA PROTECCIÓN
DIVINA

SOIR
SE REPOSER SUR LE SOIN ET LA PROTECTION
DE DIEU

O my God, my Master, the Goal of my desire! This, Thy servant, seeketh to sleep in the shelter of Thy mercy, and to repose beneath the canopy of Thy grace, imploring Thy care and Thy protection.

I beg of Thee, O my Lord, by Thine eye that sleepeth not, to guard mine eyes from beholding aught beside Thee. Strengthen, then, their vision that they may discern Thy signs, and behold the Horizon of Thy Revelation. Thou art He before the revelations of Whose omnipotence the quintessence of power hath trembled.

No God is there but Thee, the Almighty, the All-Subduing, the Unconditioned.

—BAHÁ'U'LLÁH

¡Oh mi Dios, mi Maestro, y el Objeto de mi deseo! Este siervo tuyo desea dormir al amparo de tu misericordia, y reposar bajo el dosel de tu gracia, implorando tu cuidado y tu protección.

Yo Te ruego, oh mi Señor, por tu ojo que no duerme, que guardes los míos para que no miren a otro fuera de Ti. Fortalece, pues, su visión, para que puedan distinguir tus signos y contemplar el horizonte de tu Revelación. Tú eres Aquel, ante cuya omnipotencia, al revelarse, la quintaesencia del poder se ha estremecido.

No hay Dios sino Tú, el Todopoderoso, el que Todo lo Subyuga, el Libre.

—BAHÁ'U'LLÁH

Ô mon Dieu, mon Maître, but de mon désir !
Voici ton serviteur qui aspire à s'endormir à l'ombre de ta miséricorde et à reposer sous le ciel de ta grâce, implorant ta sollicitude et ta protection.

Je te prie, ô mon Seigneur, par ton œil qui ne dort point, d'empêcher mes yeux de regarder qui que ce soit en dehors de toi. Fortifie donc leur pouvoir de perception, afin que je puisse discerner tes signes et contempler l'horizon de ta révélation. Tu es celui dont l'omnipotence, en se révélant, a ébranlé la quintessence du pouvoir.

Il n'est pas d'autre dieu que toi, le Puissant, le Victorieux, l'Absolu.

—BAHÁ'U'LLÁH

In a letter written on his behalf, Shoghi Effendi has said that the believers are free to choose one of the three daily obligatory prayers but that they must recite one of them, using the directions that accompany the prayer chosen.

DAILY OBLIGATORY PRAYERS

En una carta escrita en su nombre, Shoghi Effendi ha dicho que los creyentes están libres para elegir una de las tres oraciones obligatorias diarias pero que deben recitar una de ellas, haciendo uso de las instrucciones que acompañan a la oración escogida.

ORACIONES OBLIGATORIAS DIARIAS

Dans une lettre écrite de sa part, Shoghi Effendi a dit que le croyant était libre de choisir une des prières journalières obligatoires mais qu'il devait en réciter une chaque jour en tenant compte des indications précises qui l'accompagnent.

PRIÈRES JOURNALIÈRES OBLIGATOIRES

LONG
OBLIGATORY
PRAYER

———

LONG OBLIGATORY PRAYER
TO BE RECITED ONCE IN TWENTY-FOUR HOURS

Whoso wisheth to recite this prayer, let him stand up and turn unto God, and, as he standeth in his place, let him gaze to the right and to the left, as if awaiting the mercy of his Lord, the Most Merciful, the Compassionate. Then let him say:

O Thou Who art the Lord of all names and the Maker of the heavens! I beseech Thee by them Who are the Daysprings of Thine invisible Essence, the Most Exalted, the All-Glorious, to make of my prayer a fire that will burn away the veils which have shut me out from Thy beauty, and a light that will lead me unto the ocean of Thy Presence.

Let him then raise his hands in supplication toward God—blessed and exalted be He—and say:

O Thou the Desire of the world and the Beloved of the nations! Thou seest me turning toward Thee, and rid of all attachment to anyone save Thee, and clinging to Thy cord, through whose movement the whole creation hath been stirred up. I am Thy servant, O my Lord, and the son of Thy servant. Behold me standing ready to do Thy will and Thy desire, and wishing naught else except Thy good pleasure. I implore Thee by the Ocean of Thy mercy and the Daystar of Thy grace to do with Thy servant as Thou willest and pleasest. By Thy might which is far above all mention and praise! Whatsoever is revealed by Thee is the desire of my heart and the beloved of my soul. O God, my God! Look not upon my hopes and my doings, nay rather look upon Thy will that hath encompassed the heavens and the earth. By Thy Most Great Name, O Thou Lord of all nations! I have desired only what Thou didst desire, and love only what Thou dost love.

Let him then kneel, and bowing his forehead to the ground, let him say:

Exalted art Thou above the description of anyone save Thyself, and the comprehension of aught else except Thee.

Let him then stand and say:

Make my prayer, O my Lord, a fountain of living waters whereby I may live as long as Thy sovereignty endureth, and may make mention of Thee in every world of Thy worlds.

Let him again raise his hands in supplication, and say:

O Thou in separation from Whom hearts and souls have melted, and by the fire of Whose love the whole world hath been set aflame! I implore Thee by Thy Name through which Thou hast subdued the whole creation, not to withhold from me that which is with Thee, O Thou Who rulest over all men! Thou seest, O my Lord, this stranger hastening to his most exalted home beneath the canopy of Thy majesty and within the precincts of Thy mercy; and this transgressor seeking the ocean of Thy forgiveness; and this lowly one the court of Thy glory; and this poor creature the orient of Thy wealth. Thine is the authority to command whatsoever Thou willest. I bear witness that Thou art to be praised in Thy doings, and to be obeyed in Thy behests, and to remain unconstrained in Thy bidding.

Let him then raise his hands, and repeat three times the Greatest Name.[1] Let him then bend down with hands

---

1. Alláh-u-Abhá.

resting on the knees before God—blessed and exalted be He—and say:

Thou seest, O my God, how my spirit hath been stirred up within my limbs and members, in its longing to worship Thee, and in its yearning to remember Thee and extol Thee; how it testifieth to that whereunto the Tongue of Thy Commandment hath testified in the kingdom of Thine utterance and the heaven of Thy knowledge. I love, in this state, O my Lord, to beg of Thee all that is with Thee, that I may demonstrate my poverty, and magnify Thy bounty and Thy riches, and may declare my powerlessness, and manifest Thy power and Thy might.

Let him then stand and raise his hands twice in supplication, and say:

There is no God but Thee, the Almighty, the All-Bountiful. There is no God but Thee, the Ordainer, both in the beginning and in the end. O God, my God! Thy forgiveness hath emboldened me, and Thy mercy hath strengthened me, and Thy call hath

awakened me, and Thy grace hath raised me up and led me unto Thee. Who, otherwise, am I that I should dare to stand at the gate of the city of Thy nearness, or set my face toward the lights that are shining from the heaven of Thy will? Thou seest, O my Lord, this wretched creature knocking at the door of Thy grace, and this evanescent soul seeking the river of everlasting life from the hands of Thy bounty. Thine is the command at all times, O Thou Who art the Lord of all names; and mine is resignation and willing submission to Thy will, O Creator of the heavens!

Let him then raise his hands thrice, and say:

Greater is God than every great one!

Let him then kneel and, bowing his forehead to the ground, say:

Too high art Thou for the praise of those who are nigh unto Thee to ascend unto the heaven of Thy nearness, or for the birds of the hearts of them who are devoted to Thee to attain to the door of Thy gate. I testify that Thou hast been sanctified above all attributes and holy above all names. No God is there but Thee, the Most Exalted, the All-Glorious.

Let him then seat himself and say:

I testify unto that whereunto have testified all created things, and the Concourse on high, and the inmates of the all-highest Paradise, and beyond them the Tongue of Grandeur itself from the all-glorious Horizon, that Thou art God, that there is no God but Thee, and that He Who hath been manifested is the Hidden Mystery, the Treasured Symbol, through Whom the letters B and E (Be) have been joined and knit together. I testify that it is He Whose name hath been set down by the Pen of the Most High, and Who hath been mentioned in the Books of God, the Lord of the Throne on high and of earth below.

Let him then stand erect and say:

O Lord of all being and Possessor of all things visible and invisible! Thou dost perceive my tears and the sighs I utter, and hearest my groaning, and my wailing, and the lamentation of my heart. By Thy might! My trespasses have kept me back from drawing

nigh unto Thee; and my sins have held me far from the court of Thy holiness. Thy love, O my Lord, hath enriched me, and separation from Thee hath destroyed me, and remoteness from Thee hath consumed me. I entreat Thee by Thy footsteps in this wilderness, and by the words "Here am I. Here am I" which Thy chosen Ones have uttered in this immensity, and by the breaths of Thy Revelation, and the gentle winds of the Dawn of Thy Manifestation, to ordain that I may gaze on Thy beauty and observe whatsoever is in Thy Book.

Let him then repeat the Greatest Name thrice, and bend down with hands resting on the knees, and say:

Praise be to Thee, O my God, that Thou hast aided me to remember Thee and to praise Thee, and hast made known unto me Him Who is the Dayspring of Thy signs, and hast caused me to bow down before Thy Lordship, and humble myself before Thy Godhead, and to acknowledge that which hath been uttered by the Tongue of Thy grandeur.

Let him then rise and say:

O God, my God! My back is bowed by the burden of my sins, and my heedlessness hath destroyed me. Whenever I ponder my evil doings and Thy benevolence, my heart melteth within me, and my blood boileth in my veins. By Thy Beauty, O Thou the Desire of the world! I blush to lift up my face to Thee, and my longing hands are ashamed to stretch forth toward the heaven of Thy bounty. Thou seest, O my God, how my tears prevent me from remembering Thee and from extolling Thy virtues, O Thou the Lord of the Throne on high and of earth below! I implore Thee by the signs of Thy Kingdom and the mysteries of Thy Dominion to do with Thy loved ones as becometh Thy bounty, O Lord of all being, and is worthy of Thy grace, O King of the seen and the unseen!

Let him then repeat the Greatest Name thrice, and kneel with his forehead to the ground, and say:

Praise be unto Thee, O our God, that Thou hast sent down unto us that which draweth us nigh unto Thee, and supplieth us with every good thing sent down by Thee in Thy Books and Thy Scriptures.

Protect us, we beseech Thee, O my Lord, from the hosts of idle fancies and vain imaginations. Thou, in truth, art the Mighty, the All-Knowing.

Let him then raise his head, and seat himself, and say:

I testify, O my God, to that whereunto Thy chosen Ones have testified, and acknowledge that which the inmates of the all-highest Paradise and those who have circled round Thy mighty Throne have acknowledged. The kingdoms of earth and heaven are Thine, O Lord of the worlds!

—BAHÁ'U'LLÁH

ORACIÓN
OBLIGATORIA
LARGA

―――――

ORACIÓN OBLIGATORIA LARGA
PARA SER RECITADA CADA VEINTICUATRO HORAS

Quien desee recitar esta oración, debe ponerse de pie, dirigiéndose a Dios, y permaneciendo en su lugar, debe mirar a derecha e izquierda, como si esperase la misericordia de su Señor, el Compasivo. Luego debe decir:

¡Oh Tú Quien eres el Señor de todos los nombres y el Hacedor de los cielos! Te suplico por aquellos que son las auroras de tu invisible Esencia, el Más Exaltado, el Todo Glorioso, que hagas de mi oración un fuego que consuma los velos que me han apartado de tu belleza y una luz que me conduzca hacia el océano de tu Presencia.

Luego, levantando las manos en actitud de súplica hacia Dios, bendito y exaltado sea Él, debe decir:

¡Oh Tú, Deseo del mundo y Amado de las naciones! Tú me ves volviéndome hacia Ti, libre de todo apego a otro que no seas Tú, y aferrándome a tu cordón, por cuyo movimiento ha sido conmovida toda la creación. Soy tu siervo, oh mi Señor, y el hijo de tu siervo. Heme aquí, decidido a hacer tu voluntad y tu deseo, y anhelando solo tu complacencia. Te imploro, por el océano de tu misericordia y el sol de tu gracia, que procedas con tu siervo de acuerdo con tu voluntad y deseo. ¡Por tu poder, que está por sobre toda mención y alabanza! Todo lo que sea revelado por Ti es el deseo de mi corazón y lo amado por mi alma. ¡Oh Dios, mi Dios! No consideres mis esperanzas ni mis actos; antes bien, considera tu voluntad, que ha abarcado los cielos y la tierra. ¡Por tu Más Grande Nombre, oh Tú Señor de todas las naciones! He deseado solamente lo que Tú deseaste, y amo solamente lo que Tú amas.

Luego, arrodillándose e inclinando la frente hasta el suelo, debe decir:

Exaltado eres sobre la descripción de cualquiera que no seas Tú, y la comprensión de otro fuera de Ti.

Luego, poniéndose de pie, debe decir:

Haz de mi oración, oh mi Señor, una fuente de aguas vivientes, con las cuales pueda yo vivir tanto como perdure tu soberanía, y hacer mención de Ti en cada mundo de tus mundos.

Levantando nuevamente las manos en actitud de súplica, debe decir:

¡Oh Tú por cuya separación los corazones y las almas se han consumido, y por el fuego de cuyo amor todo el mundo se ha encendido! ¡Te imploro por tu Nombre, por medio del cual Tú has subyugado a la creación entera, que no me prives de lo que hay junto a Ti, oh Tú que reinas sobre todos los hombres! Tú ves, oh mi Señor, a este extraño apresurándose hacia su más exaltado hogar, bajo el dosel de tu majestad y dentro de los recintos de tu merced; a este transgresor anhelando el océano de tu perdón; a este humilde ser ansiando la corte de tu gloria; y a esta pobre criatura buscando el oriente de tu riqueza. Tuya es la autoridad para ordenar todo lo que sea tu voluntad. Atestiguo que Tú debes ser alabado por tus hechos, obedecido en tus mandatos, y permanecer libre en tus órdenes.

Luego, debe levantar las manos, y repetir tres veces el Más Grande Nombre.[1] A continuación, debe inclinarse con las manos sobre las rodillas, ante Dios, bendito y exaltado sea Él, y decir:

---

1. Alláh-u-Abhá.

Tú ves, oh mi Dios, cómo mi espíritu ha sido conmovido dentro de mis extremidades y miembros, en su ansia por adorarte y ensalzarte, cómo da testimonio de lo que la lengua de tu mandamiento ha atestiguado en el reino de tu palabra y en el cielo de tu conocimiento. Cuánto amo pedirte en este estado, oh mi Señor, todo lo que Tú posees, para demostrar mi pobreza y magnificar tu generosidad y tus riquezas, para declarar mi impotencia y manifestar tu fuerza y poder.

Luego, poniéndose de pie y levantando las manos dos veces en actitud de súplica, debe decir:

No hay Dios sino Tú, el Todopoderoso, el Todo Generoso. No hay Dios sino Tú, el Ordenador, tanto en el principio como en el fin. ¡Oh Dios, mi Dios! Tu perdón me ha infundido valor y tu misericordia me ha fortalecido, tu llamado me ha despertado y tu gracia me ha elevado y me ha conducido hacia Ti. De no ser así, ¿quién soy yo, para atreverme a permanecer ante la puerta de la ciudad de tu cercanía, o fijar mi rostro en las luces que brillan en el cielo de tu voluntad? Tú ves, oh mi Señor, a esta desdichada

criatura, llamando a la puerta de tu gracia, y a esta alma efímera, anhelando el río de vida eterna de manos de tu generosidad. ¡Tuyo es el mandato en todo tiempo, oh Tú Quien eres el Señor de todos los nombres, y mía es la resignación y voluntaria submisión a tu voluntad, oh Creador de los cielos!

Luego, levantando las manos tres veces, debe decir:

¡Dios es el Más Grande de todos los grandes!

Luego, arrodillándose e inclinando la frente hasta el suelo, debe decir:

Demasiado alto eres Tú para que la alabanza de aquellos que están cerca de Ti ascienda al cielo de tu cercanía, o para que los pájaros de los corazones de quienes están consagrados a Ti, alcancen la entrada de tu puerta. Atestiguo que Tú has sido santificado más allá de todo atributo y consagrado por sobre todo nombre. No hay Dios sino Tú, el Más Exaltado, el Todo Glorioso.

Luego, sentándose, debe decir:

Atestiguo lo que han atestiguado todas las cosas

creadas, el Concurso de lo alto, los moradores del más elevado Paraíso, y más allá de ellos la misma Lengua de Grandeza, desde el Horizonte todo glorioso, que Tú eres Dios, que no hay Dios sino Tú, y que Aquel Quien ha sido manifiesto es el Misterio Oculto, el Símbolo Atesorado, por medio de Quien se han unido y enlazado las letras S y E (Sé). Atestiguo que es Él cuyo nombre ha sido señalado por la Pluma del Altísimo y Quien ha sido mencionado en los Libros de Dios, el Señor del Trono en lo alto y de aquí en la tierra.

Luego, irguiéndose, debe decir:

¡Oh Señor de toda la existencia y Poseedor de todo lo visible e invisible! Tú percibes mis lágrimas y los suspiros que profiero, oyes mi gemido, mi sollozo y el lamento de mi corazón. ¡Por tu poder! Mis transgresiones me han impedido acercarme a Ti, y mis pecados me han retenido lejos de la corte de tu santidad. Tu amor, oh mi Señor, me ha enriquecido; la separación de Ti me ha destruido, y el alejamiento de Ti me ha consumido. Te suplico, por tus pasos en este desierto y por las palabras: "Aquí estoy, aquí

estoy", que tus elegidos han pronunciado en esta inmensidad, por los alientos de tu Revelación y las suaves brisas del Amanecer de tu Manifestación, que ordenes pueda yo contemplar tu belleza y observar todo lo que está en tu Libro.

Luego, debe repetir el Más Grande Nombre tres veces, e inclinándose con las manos sobre las rodillas, debe decir:

Alabado seas, oh mi Dios, por haberme ayudado a recordarte y alabarte; por haberme hecho conocer a Aquel Quien es la Aurora de tus signos e inclinarme ante tu Señorío, humillarme ante tu Deidad y reconocer lo que ha sido pronunciado por la Lengua de tu grandeza.

Luego, levantándose, debe decir:

¡Oh Dios, mi Dios! Mi espalda está inclinada por la carga de mis pecados, y mi negligencia me ha destruido. Cada vez que pienso en mis malos actos y en tu benevolencia, mi corazón se consume dentro de mí, y la sangre hierve en mis venas. ¡Por tu Belleza, oh Tú el Deseo del mundo! Me ruborizo al dirigir

mi rostro hacia Ti, y mis manos anhelantes
se avergüenzan al extenderse hacia el cielo de tu
generosidad. Tú ves, oh mi Dios, cómo las lágrimas
me impiden recordarte y ensalzar tus virtudes, ¡oh Tú
Señor del Trono en lo alto y de aquí en la tierra!
¡Te imploro por los signos de tu Reino y los misterios
de tu Dominio que procedas con tus amados como
sea propio de tu generosidad, oh Señor de todo
lo existente, y sea digno de tu gracia, oh Rey de
lo visible y lo invisible!

*Luego, debe repetir el Más Grande Nombre tres
veces, y arrodillándose con la frente hasta el suelo,
debe decir:*

Alabado seas, oh nuestro Dios, ya que Tú nos has
enviado aquello que nos acerca a Ti, y nos provees con
todo lo bueno enviado por Ti en tus Libros y en tus
Escrituras. Te suplicamos, oh mi Señor, que nos
protejas de las huestes de vanas fantasías y ociosas
imaginaciones. Tú, en verdad, eres el Poderoso,
el Omnisciente.

Luego, levantando la cabeza y sentándose, debe decir:

Atestiguo, oh mi Dios, aquello que tus elegidos
han atestiguado, y reconozco lo que los moradores del
más alto Paraíso, y aquellos que han circundado
alrededor de tu poderoso Trono, han reconocido.
¡Los reinos de la tierra y del cielo son tuyos, oh Señor
de los mundos!

—*BAHÁ'U'LLÁH*

LONGUE
PRIÈRE
OBLIGATOIRE

———

LONGUE PRIÈRE OBLIGATOIRE
À DIRE UNE FOIS CHAQUE JOUR

Pour dire cette prière, se tenir debout, se tourner vers Dieu puis, sans changer de place, regarder à droite et à gauche comme pour chercher la miséricorde du Seigneur le Très-Miséricordieux, le Compatissant, et dire :

Ô toi qui es le Seigneur de tous les noms et le Créateur des cieux ! Je te supplie par ceux qui sont les aurores de ton invisible Essence, la Très-Glorieuse, la Sublime, de faire de ma prière un feu capable de consumer les voiles qui m'ont séparé de ta beauté, et une lumière qui me conduise vers l'océan de ta présence.

Élever les mains en signe de supplication vers Dieu— béni et glorifié soit-Il—et dire :

Ô Toi le Désir du monde, le Bien-Aimé des nations ! Tu me vois tourné vers toi, libéré de tout attachement à ce qui n'est pas toi et accroché à ta corde dont le mouvement a remué la création tout entière. Je suis ton serviteur ô mon Seigneur et le fils de ton serviteur. Me voici prêt à accomplir ta volonté et ton désir, et je ne souhaite rien d'autre que ton bon plaisir. Je t'implore, par l'océan de ta miséricorde et l'Étoile du Matin de ta grâce, d'employer ton serviteur comme tu voudras et comme il te plaira. Par ta puissance qui surpasse de loin toute mention et louange, tout ce que tu révèles est le vœu de mon cœur et le désir de mon âme.

Ô Dieu, mon Dieu ! Ne tiens compte ni de mes espoirs ni de mes actes, mais bien de ta volonté qui a englobé les cieux et la terre. Par ton très Grand Nom, ô toi Seigneur de toutes les nations ! Je n'ai voulu que ce que tu as voulu, et je n'aime que ce que tu aimes.

S'agenouiller et, baissant le front vers la terre, dire :

Tu es infiniment élevé au-dessus de toute description sauf de ta description et de la compréhension de tout autre que toi.

Se lever alors et dire :

Fais que ma prière, ô mon Seigneur, soit une fontaine d'eau vive qui me permette de vivre tant que durera ta souveraineté, et de te mentionner dans chacun de tes mondes.

Lever à nouveau des mains suppliantes et dire :

Ô toi, dont la séparation a consumé les cœurs et les âmes, et dont le feu de l'amour a embrasé le monde entier, je t'implore, par ton nom qui a conquis toute la création, de ne point me refuser ce qui est à toi, ô toi qui gouvernes tous les hommes ! Tu vois, ô mon Seigneur, cet étranger se hâtant vers sa très glorieuse demeure, sous le dais de ta majesté, dans le sanctuaire de ta miséricorde, ce transgresseur à la recherche de l'océan de ton pardon, cet humble se dirigeant vers les parvis de ta gloire, cette pauvre créature en quête du soleil levant de ta richesse. C'est à toi qu'appartiennent toute autorité et tout commandement. Je témoigne qu'il convient de te louer en tes actes, d'obéir à tes ordres, et j'atteste qu'aucune contrainte ne doit t'influencer dans tes commandements.

Lever alors les mains et répéter trois fois le très Grand Nom.[1] S'incliner ensuite devant Dieu—béni et loué soit—Il—, poser les mains sur les genoux et dire :

---

1. « Alláh-u-Abhá »

Tu vois, ô mon Dieu, combien tout mon être a été ébranlé par le vif désir de t'adorer et par l'ardeur à mentionner ton nom et à te louer; Tu vois comment mon esprit a affirmé ce que la langue de ton commandement avait certifié dans le royaume de ta parole et au ciel de ta connaissance. Dans cet état d'esprit, j'aime à te demander, ô mon Seigneur, tout ce qui est à toi, afin de prouver ma pauvreté, glorifier ta bonté et ta richesse, avouer mon impuissance et démontrer ton pouvoir et ta force.

Se redresser ensuite, lever deux fois les mains en signe de supplication et dire :

Il n'est pas d'autre dieu que toi, le Tout-Puissant, l'infiniment Généreux. Il n'y a pas d'autre dieu que toi, l'Ordonnateur au commencement et à la fin. Ô Dieu, mon Dieu, ta clémence m'a enhardi et ta miséricorde m'a fortifié; ton appel m'a réveillé, ta grâce m'a élevé et conduit jusqu'à toi. Que serais-je autrement, et comment oserais-je me tenir à l'entrée de la cité de ton approche, ou lever mon visage vers les lumières qui luisent du ciel de ta volonté ? Tu vois, ô mon Seigneur, cette misérable créature frapper à la porte de ta grâce, cette âme éphémère qui cherche la

rivière de vie éternelle s'écoulant des mains de ta générosité. En tout temps le commandement t'appartient ô toi qui es le Seigneur de tous les noms; pour moi sont la résignation et la soumission de bon gré à ta volonté, ô Créateur des cieux.

Lever trois fois les mains en disant :

Dieu est plus grand que tous les grands.

S'agenouiller ensuite et, inclinant le front vers le sol, dire :

Tu es trop élevé pour que la louange de ceux qui sont proches de toi puisse s'élever jusqu'au ciel de ta présence ou pour que les oiseaux des cœurs de ceux qui te sont dévoués atteignent le seuil de ta porte. J'atteste que tu as été sanctifié au-delà de tout attribut et que ta sainteté est au-dessus de toute expression. Il n'est pas d'autre dieu que toi, le Plus-Élevé, l'infiniment Glorieux.

Puis s'asseoir et dire :

Ainsi qu'en a témoigné tout ce qui est créé: l'assemblée céleste, les habitants du paradis suprême et, au-delà d'eux, de l'horizon de gloire, la Langue de grandeur elle-même, j'atteste que tu es Dieu, qu'il n'y a pas d'autre dieu que toi, et que celui qui a été manifesté est le mystère caché, le symbole précieux par qui les lettres SOIS (« sois ») ont été jointes et liées. J'atteste que c'est Lui dont le nom a été inscrit par la plume du Très-Haut, et qui a été mentionné dans les livres de Dieu, le Seigneur du trône céleste et de la terre.

Se mettre debout et dire :

Ô Seigneur de tous les êtres et Possesseur de toutes choses visibles et invisibles ! Tu vois sûrement mes larmes, tu perçois mes soupirs, tu entends mes plaintes, mes gémissements et les lamentations de mon cœur. Par ta puissance ! Mes offenses m'ont empêché de m'approcher de toi, et mes péchés m'ont éloigné des cours de ta sainteté. Ton amour, ô mon Seigneur, m'a enrichi; me séparer de toi m'a consumé, Je te supplie, par les traces de tes pas dans ce désert et par ces mots : « me voici, me voici », prononcés par tes élus dans cette immensité, et par les souffles de ta révélation et les brises légères de l'Aurore de ta manifestation, d'ordonner qu'il me soit permis de

contempler ta Beauté et d'observer tout ce qui est contenu dans ton livre.

Répéter trois fois le très Grand Nom, s'incliner, les mains posées sur les genoux, et dire :

Loué sois-tu, ô mon Dieu, pour m'avoir aidé à me souvenir de toi et à te louer, pour m'avoir fait connaître celui qui est l'Aurore de tes signes, pour m'avoir fait m'incliner devant ta souveraineté, devenir humble devant ta Divinité et reconnaître ce qui a été prononcé par la Langue de ta grandeur.

Se mettre debout et dire :

Ô Dieu, mon Dieu, Mon dos s'est courbé sous le poids de mes péchés et ma négligence m'a anéanti. Quand je médite sur mes mauvaises actions et sur ta bienveillance, mon cœur s'attendrit et mon sang se glace dans mes veines. Par ta beauté, ô toi qui es le Désiré du monde ! Je rougis de lever mon visage vers toi, et j'ai honte de tendre avec ardeur des mains suppliantes vers le ciel de ta bonté. Tu vois, ô mon Dieu, combien mes larmes m'empêchent de te mentionner et d'exalter tes vertus, ô toi le Seigneur du trône céleste et de la terre. Je t'implore, par les signes de ton royaume et les mystères de ton empire, d'agir envers tes bien-aimés comme il sied à ta bonté, ô Seigneur de tous les êtres, et selon ce qui convient à ta grâce, ô Roi du visible et de l'invisible !

Répéter ensuite trois fois le Très Grand Nom, s'agenouiller et, baissant le front vers la terre, dire :

Loué sois-tu, ô notre Dieu, pour avoir fait descendre sur nous ce qui nous rapproche de toi, et pour nous procurer tous les biens promis par toi dans tes livres et tes Écritures. Protège-nous, nous t'en supplions, ô Seigneur, des armées des folles illusions et des vaines imaginations. Tu es, en vérité, le Puissant, l'Omniscient.

Se relever alors, s'asseoir et dire :

J'atteste, ô mon Dieu, ce que tes élus ont affirmé, et je reconnais ce qu'ont accepté les habitants du très haut paradis ainsi que ceux qui gravitent autour de ton trône de puissance. Les royaumes de la terre et du ciel sont à toi, ô Seigneur des mondes !

—*BAHÁ'U'LLÁH*

MEDIUM
OBLIGATORY
PRAYER

———

ORACIÓN
OBLIGATORIA
MEDIANA

———

PRIÈRE
OBLIGATOIRE
MOYENNE

MEDIUM OBLIGATORY PRAYER
TO BE RECITED DAILY,
IN THE MORNING, AT NOON, AND IN THE EVENING

The Synopsis and Codification of the Kitáb-i-Aqdas explains that, in connection with the daily obligatory prayers, morning means the period between sunrise and noon, noon means the period between noon and sunset, and evening means from sunset until two hours after sunset.

Whoso wisheth to pray, let him wash his hands, and while he washeth, let him say:

Strengthen my hand, O my God, that it may take hold of Thy Book with such steadfastness that the hosts of the world shall have no power over it. Guard it, then, from meddling with whatsoever doth not belong unto it. Thou art, verily, the Almighty, the Most Powerful.

And while washing his face, let him say:

I have turned my face unto Thee, O my Lord! Illumine it with the light of Thy countenance. Protect it, then, from turning to anyone but Thee.

Then let him stand up, and facing the Qiblih (Point of Adoration, i.e., Bahjí, 'Akká), let him say:

God testifieth that there is none other God but Him. His are the kingdoms of Revelation and of creation. He, in truth, hath manifested Him Who is the Dayspring of Revelation, Who conversed on Sinai, through Whom the Supreme Horizon hath been made to shine, and the Lote-Tree beyond which there is no passing hath spoken, and through Whom the call hath been proclaimed unto all who are in heaven and on earth: "Lo, the All-Possessing is come. Earth and heaven, glory and dominion are God's, the Lord of all men, and the Possessor of the Throne on high and of earth below!"

Let him, then, bend down, with hands resting on the knees, and say:

Exalted art Thou above my praise and the praise of anyone beside me, above my description and the description of all who are in heaven and all who are on earth!

Then, standing with open hands, palms upward toward the face, let him say:

Disappoint not, O my God, him that hath, with beseeching fingers, clung to the hem of Thy mercy and Thy grace, O Thou Who of those who show mercy art the Most Merciful!

Let him, then, be seated and say:

I bear witness to Thy unity and Thy oneness, and that Thou art God, and that there is none other God beside Thee. Thou hast, verily, revealed Thy Cause, fulfilled Thy Covenant, and opened wide the door of Thy grace to all that dwell in heaven and on earth. Blessing and peace, salutation and glory, rest upon Thy loved ones, whom the changes and chances of the world have not deterred from turning unto Thee, and who have given their all, in the hope of obtaining that which is with Thee. Thou art, in truth, the Ever-Forgiving, the All-Bountiful.

(If anyone choose to recite instead of the long verse these words: "God testifieth that there is none other God but Him, the Help in Peril, the Self-Subsisting," it would be sufficient. And likewise, it would suffice were he, while seated, to choose to recite these words: "I bear witness to Thy unity and Thy oneness, and that Thou art God, and that there is none other God beside Thee.")

—BAHÁ'U'LLÁH

ORACIÓN OBLIGATORIA MEDIANA
PARA RECITAR DIARIAMENTE, POR LA MAÑANA, AL MEDIODÍA, Y AL ATARDECER

La Sinopsis y Codificación del Kitáb-i-Aqdas explica que, en relación a las oraciones obligatorias diarias, la mañana significa el período entre el amanecer y el mediodía, el mediodía significa el período entre el mediodía y la puesta del sol, y la tarde está entre la puesta del sol y dos horas despues de la puesta del sol.

Quienquiera desee orar, debe lavarse las manos y, mientras se las lava, decir:

Fortalece mi mano, oh mi Dios, para que se aferre a tu Libro con tal firmeza que las huestes del mundo no tengan poder sobre ella. Cuídala, entonces, para que no se ocupe de aquello que no le sea propio.

Tú eres, verdaderamente, el Todopoderoso, el Omnipotente.

Y mientras se lava la cara debe decir:

¡He vuelto mi rostro hacia Ti, oh mi Señor! Ilumínalo con la luz de tu semblante. Protégelo, pues, para que no se vuelva hacia otro sino hacia Ti.

Luego, poniéndose de pie, en dirección al Qiblih (Punto de adoración en Bahjí, 'Akká), debe decir:

Dios atestigua que no hay Dios sino Él. Suyos son los reinos de la Revelación y de la creación. Él, en verdad, ha manifestado a Aquel Quien es la Aurora de la Revelación, Quien conversó en el Sinaí, por medio de Quien ha brillado el Supremo Horizonte, y ha hablado el Árbol del Loto, más allá del cual no hay paso, por medio de Quien ha sido proclamado a todos los que están en el cielo y en la tierra el llamado: "He aquí, el Todo Poseedor ha llegado! ¡La tierra y el cielo, la gloria y el dominio son de Dios, Señor de todos los hombres, y Poseedor del Trono en lo alto y de aquí en la tierra!"

Luego, inclinándose y con las manos sobre las rodillas, debe decir:

¡Exaltado eres Tú por encima de mi alabanza y la alabanza de cualquier otro que no sea yo, por encima de mi descripción y la descripción de todos los que están en el cielo y todos los que están en la tierra!

Luego, de pie y con las manos abiertas con las palmas enfrentando al rostro, debe decir:

¡No decepciones, oh mi Dios, a quien con dedos suplicantes, se ha aferrado al borde de tu misericordia y gracia, oh Tú Quien eres el Más Misericordioso entre aquellos que muestran misericordia!

Luego, sentándose, debe decir:

Soy testigo de tu unidad y de tu unicidad, de que Tú eres Dios y que no hay Dios sino Tú. Verdaderamente, Tú has revelado tu Causa, cumplido tu Convenio y has abierto de par en par la puerta de tu gracia a todos los que habitan en el cielo y en la tierra. Bendición y paz, salutaciones y gloria sean para tus amados, a quienes ni los cambios ni azares del mundo les han impedido volverse hacia Ti, quienes han dado todo con la esperanza de obtener aquello que hay junto a Ti. Tú eres, en verdad, el Siempre Perdonador, el Todo Generoso.

Si se desea recitar en lugar del largo verso las siguientes palabras: "Dios atestigua que no hay Dios sino Él, el que Ayuda en el Peligro, Quien Subsiste por Sí Mismo", sería suficiente. Bastaría también, si al estar sentado recitara estas palabras: "Soy testigo de tu unidad y de tu unicidad, de que Tú eres Dios y que no hay Dios sino Tú".

—BAHÁ'U'LLÁH

PRIÈRE OBLIGATOIRE MOYENNE
À DIRE TROIS FOIS CHAQUE JOUR, LE MATIN, À MIDI ET LE SOIR

Dans La Synopse et codification du Kitáb-i-Aqdas il est expliqué que, en ce qui concerne les prières journalières obligatoires, le matin se réfère à la période entre le lever du soleil et midi, midi se réfère à la période entre midi et le coucher du soleil et soir veut dire du coucher du soleil jusqu'à deux heures après le coucher du soleil.

En se lavant les mains, dire :

Fortifie ma main, ô mon Dieu, pour qu'elle puisse tenir ton livre avec une fermeté telle que les armées du monde n'aient sur elle aucun pouvoir. Garde-la donc de se mêler de ce qui ne la concerne pas. Tu es, en vérité, le Puissant, l'Omnipotent.

En se lavant le visage, dire :

J'ai tourné mon visage vers toi, ô mon Dieu ! Éclaire-le de la lumière de ta face. Protège-le afin qu'il ne se tourne vers nul autre que toi.

Puis, debout, tourné vers la quiblih (point d'adoration, c'est-à-dire Bahjí, à 'Akká), dire :

Dieu atteste qu'il n'y a pas d'autre dieu que Lui. À lui sont les royaumes de la révélation et de la création. Il a, en vérité, manifesté Celui qui est l'Aube de la révélation, celui qui a conversé sur le Sinaï, celui par qui le suprême horizon a brillé, par qui l'Arbre sublime, au delà duquel il n'y a pas de passage, a parlé, et par qui a été lancé cet appel pour tous ceux qui sont au ciel et sur la terre : « Voici que le Possesseur de toutes choses est venu. La terre et le ciel, la gloire et la puissance sont à Dieu, le Seigneur de tous les hommes et le Possesseur du trône et de la terre. »

S'incliner ensuite, les mains posées sur les genoux et dire :

Exalté sois-tu au-dessus de ma louange et de la louange de tout autre, au-dessus de ma description et de celle de tous les habitants du ciel et de la terre !

Puis, debout, les mains ouvertes, les paumes levées vers le visage, dire :

Ne déçois pas, ô mon Dieu, celui qui, les mains suppliantes, s'est attaché au pan de la robe de ta miséricorde et de ta grâce, ô toi qui es le plus Miséricordieux de ceux qui pratiquent la miséricorde !

Enfin s'asseoir et dire :

J'atteste que tu es un et unique, que tu es Dieu et qu'il n'y a pas d'autre dieu qui toi. Tu as, en vérité, révélé ta cause, réalisé ton alliance et ouvert largement la porte de ta grâce à tous ceux qui habitent au ciel et sur la terre. Bénédiction et paix, salut et

gloire soient sur tes bien-aimés que les changements et vicissitudes de ce monde n'ont pas empêchés de se tourner vers toi, et qui ont abandonné tout ce qu'ils possédaient dans l'espoir d'obtenir ce qui est avec toi. Tu es, en vérité, l'éternellement Clément, le Très-Munificent.

Si on le préfère, il pourra suffire, au lieu de ce long verset, de réciter ces paroles :

Dieu atteste qu'il n'y a pas d'autre dieu qui Lui, l'Aide dans le péril, celui qui subsiste par Lui-même.

De même, après s'être assis, on peut dire ces mots :

J'atteste ton unité et ton unicité et que tu es Dieu et qu'il n'y a pas d'autre dieu que toi.

—BAHÁ'U'LLÁH

SHORT OBLIGATORY PRAYER

ORACIÓN OBLIGATORIA CORTA

COURTE PRIÈRE OBLIGATOIRE

SHORT OBLIGATORY PRAYER
TO BE RECITED ONCE IN TWENTY-FOUR HOURS, AT NOON

ORACIÓN OBLIGATORIA CORTA
PARA RECITAR CADA VEINTICUATRO HORAS, AL MEDIODÍA

COURTE PRIÈRE OBLIGATOIRE
À DIRE CHAQUE JOUR ENTRE MIDI ET LE COUCHER DU SOLEIL

The Synopsis and Codification of the Kitáb-i-Aqdas explains that, in connection with the daily obligatory prayers, noon means the period between noon and sunset.

La Sinopsis y Codificación del Kitáb-i-Aqdas explica que, en relación a las oraciones obligatorias diarias, el mediodía significa el período entre el mediodía y la puesta del sol.

Dans La Synope et codification du Kitáb-i-Aqdas il est précisé que, pour ce qui est des prières journalières obligatoires, midi veut dire entre midi et le coucher du soleil.

I bear witness, O my God, that Thou hast created me to know Thee and to worship Thee. I testify, at this moment, to my powerlessness and to Thy might, to my poverty and to Thy wealth.

There is none other God but Thee, the Help in Peril, the Self-Subsisting.

—BAHÁ'U'LLÁH

Soy testigo, oh mi Dios, de que Tú me has creado para conocerte y adorarte. Atestiguo en este momento mi impotencia y tu poder, mi pobreza y tu riqueza.

No hay otro Dios más que Tú, el que Ayuda en el Peligro, Quien Subsiste por Sí Mismo.

—BAHÁ'U'LLÁH

Je suis témoin, ô mon Dieu, que tu m'as créé pour te connaître et pour t'adorer. J'atteste en cet instant mon impuissance et ton pouvoir, ma pauvreté et ta richesse.

Il n'est pas d'autre dieu que toi, celui qui secourt dans le péril, celui qui subsiste par Lui-même.

—BAHÁ'U'LLÁH